Eucharistic Adoration for Little Ones

Written by Kimberly Fries

Illustrated by Gemma C. Mohun

First Edition: August 2020

Cover by Sue Kouma Johnson

ISBN-13: 9798678727909

O Sacrament most Holy,
O Sacrament Divine,
All praise and all thanksgiving,
Be every moment Thine.
- St. Thomas Aquinas

Go in front of a crucifix or the Blessed Sacrament.

Kneel down or sit in front of Jesus
and make the sign of the cross.

Call upon the Holy Spirit.

Thank you, Holy Spirit, for guiding me to Eucharistic Adoration.

Help me to pray and grow in love.

Jesus is truly present, Body, Blood, Soul, and Divinity in the Blessed Sacrament. Jesus may be in the tabernacle or he may be placed in the monstrance on the altar. When you come to visit him be sure to be very quiet, so that you can listen to his voice in your heart.

Go often to rest your heart upon the tabernacle.

– St. Leonie Aviat

The same Jesus that walked on earth is present to us in the Blessed Sacrament. The same Jesus that is in heaven is present in the Eucharist. He is present here on earth under the appearance of bread and wine.

Nowhere does Jesus hear our prayers and more readily than in the Blessed Sacrament.

– Blessed Henry Suzo

When we are before Jesus in the Blessed Sacrament, we know that not only Jesus is there, but also the Father and the Holy Spirit. Recognize the Father's gaze on you, the Son standing before you, and the Holy Spirit shining on you.

Every time we look at the Blessed Sacrament, our place in heaven is raised forever.

– St. Gertrude the Great

Prayer to the Father

Thank you for creating me, my family, and the world around me. Thank you for your love and for sending your Son, Jesus, so that I can someday be in heaven with you forever. Help me to do your will every day.

Prayer to the Son

Jesus, my closest friend, I want to tell you all about my day, the exciting parts and the sad parts. Give me your heart so that I can love you and everyone around me more. Teach me how to be a good and obedient child.

Prayer to the Holy Spirit

Kindle the flame of your love in my heart. Together with the Father and Son, wrap me in your love. Fill me with your gifts so that I may serve God and bring all those around me closer to you.

Prayer to Mary

Mary, Mother of Jesus, help me to recognize that your Son is truly here with me. Help me to love him as you love him. Teach me how to say "yes!" to God's will in my life. Guide me so that I can offer all my heart, soul, mind, and strength to God!

Spiritual Communion Prayer

My Jesus,

I believe that You are present in the Most Holy Sacrament. I love You above all things, and I desire to receive You into my soul. Since I cannot at this moment receive You sacramentally, come at least spiritually into my heart. I embrace You as if You were already there and unite myself wholly to You. Never permit me to be separated from You.

Amen.

It's the Hidden Jesus. I love Him so much.
— St. Francisco Marto

Divine Praises

Blessed be God.

Blessed be His Holy Name.

Blessed be Jesus Christ, true God and true Man.

Blessed be the Name of Jesus.

Blessed be His Most Sacred Heart.

Blessed be His Most Precious Blood.

Blessed be Jesus in the Most Holy Sacrament of the Altar.

Blessed be the Holy Spirit, the Paraclete.

Blessed be the great Mother of God, Mary most Holy.

Blessed be her Holy and Immaculate Conception.

Blessed be her Glorious Assumption.

Blessed be the name of Mary, Virgin and Mother.

Blessed be St. Joseph, her most chaste spouse.

Blessed be God in His Angels and in His Saints. Amen.

May the heart of Jesus, in the Most Blessed Sacrament, be praised, adored, and loved with grateful affection, at every moment, in all the tabernacles of the world, even to the end of time. Amen.

How blessed we are that Jesus is truly present anytime we enter a Catholic Church. Jesus is there for us and he longs for you to visit him.

Dear young people, the happiness you are seeking, the happiness you have a right to enjoy has a name and a face: it is Jesus of Nazareth, hidden in the Eucharist.

– Pope Benedict XVI

I love you Father,
Son, and Holy Spirit!

I love you Mary!

Thank you for the beautiful gift
of the Eucharist!

Make the
Sign of the Cross.

Collect them all!

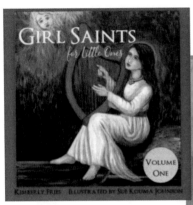

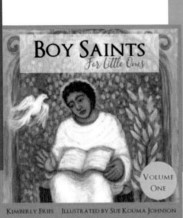

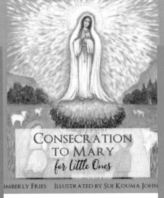

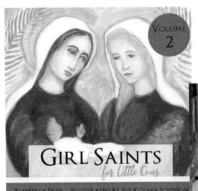

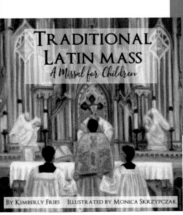

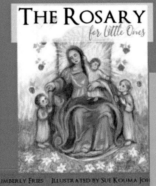

Bring Christ into your Home!

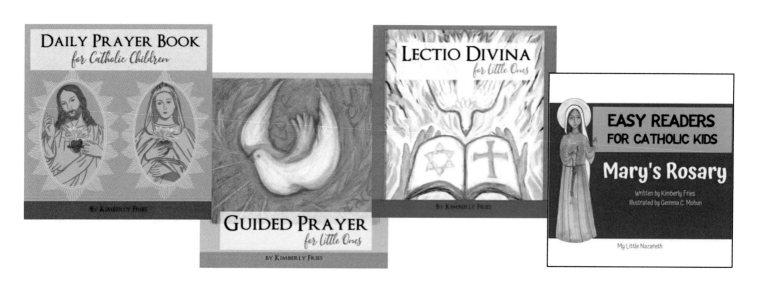

I would love to hear from you!

Please write a review at Amazon.com

Want to be the first to know about my new releases?

Follow me on Facebook, Instagram, Youtube, and my blog!
www.mylittlenazareth.com

Wholesale Prices also available!

Made in the USA
Middletown, DE
05 September 2024

60422966R00020